So, Mr. Mayor, You Want To Improve Productivity . . .

by
John Sheridan Thomas

Foreword

So, Mr. Mayor, You Want to Improve Productivity was written for the National Commission on Productivity and Work Quality by John S. Thomas, formerly Deputy Director of the Budget and productivity manager for the City of New York.

It was distributed to every local government CEO (mayors, city managers, county executives) in the nation. After these many years it is likely to be found only in their archives.

The fundamental principles of government productivity have not changed; nor has the need for continued focus on the efficient use of taxpayer funds in the performance government services. To preserve these principles, **So Mr. Mayor** re-published in a more compact and convenient format.

Several organizations were consulted during the preparation of the booklet: the American Federation of State, County and Municipal Employees; Labor-Management Relations Service of the National League of Cities, U.S. Conference of Mayors, and National Association of Counties; The Urban Institute; International City Management Association; and the Committee for Economic Development. The views contained herein do not necessarily represent an official opinion or policy of these organizations.

CONTENTS

So, Mr. Mayor, You Want to Improve Productivity...

Who's in charge of government productivity in your town, Mr. Mayor? You are, and if you don't believe it, you may turn out to be right -- after the next election. State and local governments are consuming more of the nation's resources (Figure 2); thus it is imperative to improve productivity.

Figure 2. State and Local Government's Share of the GNP is Increasing Rapidly*

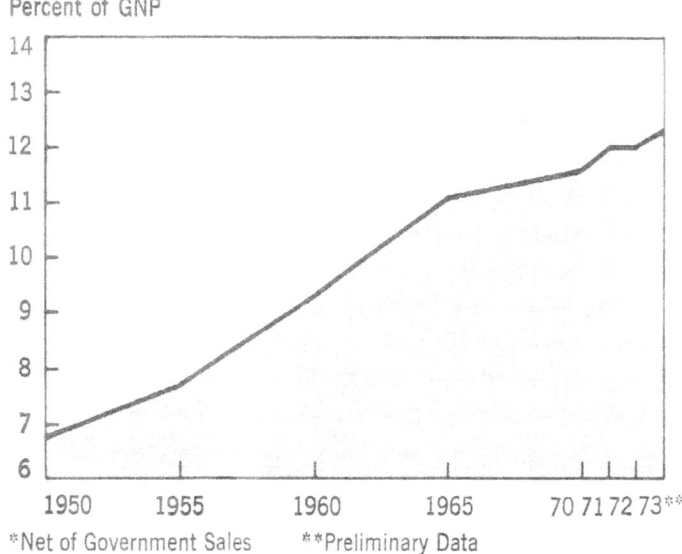

Percent of GNP

*Net of Government Sales   **Preliminary Data

Source: U.S. Department of Commerce, Bureau of Economic Analysis

Improving productivity means giving the taxpayers more services for their tax dollars, or giving them the same services for fewer tax dollars. It is the path between tax increases and service reductions. It is not easy to find, and it will not lie in exactly the same direction in every city. So we have written this booklet to help you find the path to greater productivity in your city.

Our emphasis is on organization and management. Without them, you leave productivity to chance -- which will work against you nearly as often as for you -- or to outside forces.

Without an organized and analytical approach, neither you nor the people whose support you want can ever be sure that your city is getting its money's worth.

INCREASED PRODUCTIVITY IMPROVES SERVICES AND HOLDS DOWN COSTS

We propose systematic analysis of every government department.   Don't wait for technological revolutions and don't depend solely on the imagination of your employees.

Of all the ways to address the productivity issue, systematic analysis holds the greatest promise of improvement on every front by bringing to the surface needed changes which perhaps have long gone unnoticed. And it is a means of achieving greater accountability from your managers.

There are functions in every city that have never been exposed to a methodical analysis, one that deals in depth with management, your information processing system, operational systems, and the performance of the employees.

When was the last time your building inspection or sewer maintenance work practices were analyzed in detail? Is your water department staffed by more or fewer people than those in comparable cities? How well does the productivity of the city motor pool compare with that of local commercial garages?

Most public officials don't have the answers to these questions and dozens like them because they haven't thought about their operations in the context of productivity. And they haven't used analytical staff to find out how your money is spent, how the work gets done, or what results are achieved.

A well executed, comprehensive program can improve the quality and quantity of services and hold down costs - in short raise productivity.

DON'T LEAVE PRODUCTIVITY TO CHANCE

Sustaining an organized improvement program requires dedication to productivity as a priority concern of your administration, continuing attention and hard work on the part of your managerial organization and whatever analytical staff you assign to the program. But most of all, it requires your leadership and support.

EXCERSIZE YOUR LEADERSHIP
AND LEND YOUR SUPPORT

As we proceed through this booklet, we will cite a number of opportunities and techniques for productivity improvement already proven successful in some cities.

Don't hesitate to copy others' successes. Your electorate is more interested in results then originality. But because not every example will be applicable to the unique characteristics of your city, we have tried to abstract some general principles you can apply to your situation. And this booklet tries to help you organize these principles into a productivity program.

But before we get into the details, let's take note of a few of the myths, misconceptions, and risks traditionally associated with productivity improvement.

Myths. One myth is that somehow productivity improvement is inherent in the American economic system and work ethic, so that there is no need to "program" improvement efforts. But recent events have badly shaken these assumptions. Lagging productivity coupled with rising inflationary pressure has helped retard the growth of the GNP and weakened the international competitive posture of the United States.

Productivity is a national concern; we have come to see that it is not part of the Bill of Rights. Productivity gains are the direct result of the collective actions of government, industry, and workers. And productivity gains in the public sector contribute to the national welfare as much as gains in the private sector.

As government services consume a larger and larger share of our resources it becomes imperative that public officials focus on productivity improvement.

Most public officials don't have the answers to these questions and dozens like them because they haven't thought about their operations in the context of productivity. And they haven't used analytical staff to find out how money is spent, how work is done, or what results are achieved. A well executed, comprehensive improvement program can demonstrably increase the quality and quantity of services and hold down costs, or, in short, raise productivity.

As we proceed through this booklet, we will cite a number of opportunities and techniques for productivity improvement already proven successful in some cities. Don't hesitate to copy others' successes. Your electorate is as interested in results as in originality. Not every example will be applicable to the unique characteristics of your city, so we have tried to abstract some general principles you can apply to your situation. And this booklet tries to help you organize these principles into a productivity program.

Another myth suggests that productivity is fine for manufacturing industries, whose activities are easily measured, but has little meaning for services. Just look at the wide variations in tons per man for solid waste collection from city to city, and you'll suspect that some are more productive in providing service than others (see Figure 3). In reality, there are too many examples of real productivity gains in government services to give credence to this myth.

Misconceptions. Possibly the most prevalent misconception is that organized labor opposes any effort to improve productivity. Organized labor is understandably protective of the wages and benefits won for its members at the bargaining table. Yes, there are occasional contractual provisions that may seem restrictive.

Figure 3. City to City Variations in Garbage Collection Productivity

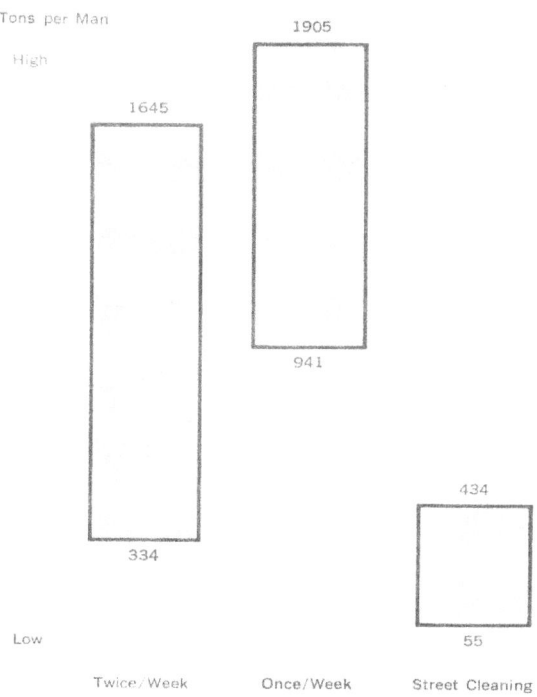

Tons per Man

High

1905

1645

941

334

434

55

Low

Twice/Week   Once/Week   Street Cleaning

Restrictive labor provisions often involve concerns about job safety or unreasonable hardship or burdens on the employee. The leaders of public employee unions who oppose productivity per se are a small minority. After all, increased productivity is rapidly becoming the key to wage increases without the unpopular measure of tax increases.

Risks. There are some risks connected with a productivity program. There is a risk of break-down in service if changes are not adequately planned or managed. Serious misunderstandings can arise in bargaining, but usually they can be avoided through careful preparation and effective communication. There is personal risk to you as mayor in terms of your credibility if you embark on a highly publicized program that ultimately yields little. On the other hand, the political risk of doing nothing about productivity is real if failure to act means deteriorating services or raising local taxes.

THE REWARDS ARE WORTH THE RISKS

If your productivity program is successful, the rewards to you personally are willing to make of them, but to the taxpayer the benefits are clear and unequivocal. Maximum productivity in municipal operations is not an option, it is an imperative. It reflects the right of every taxpayer to get every ounce of service from every dollar he provides.

Planning Your Productivity Program

Before embarking on your productivity program, you'll have to make some decisions about its scope, structure, and content.   Few if any of these decisions will be irreversible, so avoid getting bogged down in endless planning sessions, debates about administration, or organization, reporting mechanisms, philosophical concepts, and the like.

Extensive planning isn't necessary; but consider the following:

- ➢ Scope of Your Program and Selecting Priorities
- ➢ Organizing Your Program
- ➢ Resource Requirements
- ➢ Involving Labor and Others
- ➢ Role of the Chief Executive

Scope of Your Program and Selecting Priorities

There are no broad management decisions you can take which will simultaneously increase productivity on all fronts. Whatever theoretical generalizations we may make, practical productivity gains are achieved in the delivery of particular goods and services, and different problems have different solutions.

Thus, while you eventually want your productivity program to embrace all city functions, you must begin with specific operations or specific problems.

Where do you start? Remember that poor productivity is often not a visible problem. Here are some criteria for conducting your search for a good starting point:

- Operations where large numbers of employees perform essentially repetitive tasks. Improvement of such operations is likely to yield large benefits.

- Functions continually faced with large backlogs of work. The backlogs themselves are symptomatic of problems to be solved.

- Operations where visible problems exist. Improvements will also be highly visible.

- Availability of new techniques or technology already proven practical elsewhere.

- Receptivity of the operation's managers to new ideas coupled with an ability to follow through.

Productivity pertains to both goods and services, and it pertains to both quantity and quality. More service and better service are both important objectives of your program.

An increase in the number of tons of refuse collected per man-day represents a gain in productivity. So does eliminating missed collections or improving the cleanliness of your streets. Your search for a good starting point should include qualitative as well as quantitative improvements.

NOTHING SUCCEEDS LIKE SUCCESS

If at first you don't succeed, you've started in the wrong place. And you may not get to try, try again. Early failures make future efforts more difficult, if not impossible, so it is particularly important that your initial efforts succeed. And initial successes become valuable sales points in gaining the acceptance and support needed to expand your program. Thus, probability of success is perhaps the most important criterion in selecting your starting point.

Organizing Your Program

Your natural instinct may be to place the administrative responsibility for your productivity program in an existing staff organization (see Figure 4) such as budget, personnel, or labor relations. Resist that instinct. Don't delegate the responsibility for productivity, certainly not at the beginning of your program.

Productivity improvement is one of the more sensitive and difficult new programs you're likely to attempt. The very term "productivity improvement" implies criticism of present methods. So the program will require all the persuasive powers you can muster. You must show your personal determination to see the program through until others have become dedicated enough to maintain the momentum.

Keep the administration of the productivity program as close to you as possible for the first year or two and you'll increase the likelihood of success. Assign it to your deputy or assistant, or borrow the best staff assistant you can find in your government to work directly under you. His key duties will include documenting and promulgating decisions; determining reporting requirements and seeing that they are met; arranging meetings; advising you when policy decisions are necessary; and generally monitoring all activities to see that the program is moving on schedule.

FIX ADMINISTRATIVE RESPONSIBILITY

Figure 4. Organize the Program

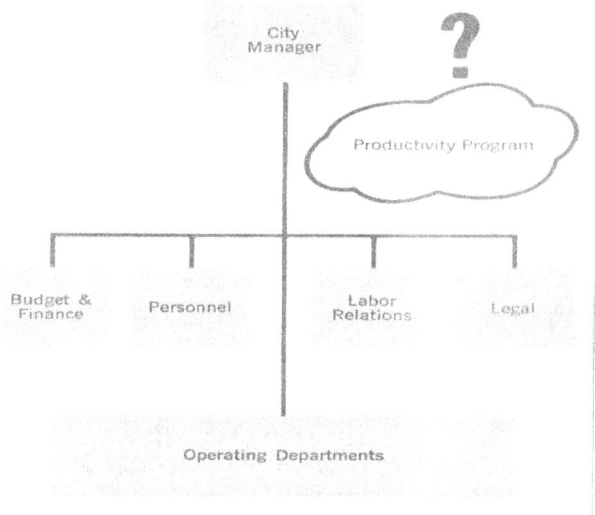

Fixing administrative responsibility in a key official directly responsible to you is the first organizational step. The second is lining up your analytical talent. The most successful productivity improvements usually result from assigning competent analysts to the program on a fulltime basis.

Every government operation should at some time be subjected to in-depth studies using the systematic techniques commonly employed by industrial engineers, systems analysts, and accountants, techniques such as work-load balancing, time study, flow-charting, and systems design.

Labor intensive operations are particularly susceptible to industrial engineering analysis. This frequently leads to improved planning, scheduling, and delivery of services. Information processing operations offer great opportunities for systems analysis and application of computer technology.

Typical targets for operations research techniques are functions that involve complex cause and effect relationships that are not clearly understood. Examples would be the impact of police deployment patterns on crime rates or the impact of housing regulations on housing availability.

LINE UP YOUR ANALYTIC TALENT

In addition to technical analytical skills, your senior analysts should possess leadership and negotiating qualities. They must demonstrate an ability to apply their technical skills to the practical problems confronting your line managers, and they must gain the confidence and respect of the line organization. The analyst whose opinion on garbage collection will be listened to is the analyst who has gone out on a garbage truck. Your analysts should serve as catalysts to stimulate serious thought and discussion within the operating organizations about ways to improve service.

As you begin to organize your program, you will need to decide whether these analysts should be part of a central organization (an Office of Productivity?) providing assistance to operating departments, or whether they should be decentralized, reporting directly to their respective department heads. An important criterion in this decision is the level of skill and experience of the analytical people. There is a severe shortage of senior analysts who can achieve success without strong organizational support. And there is considerable risk in placing junior analysts in operating departments where they may become discouraged by non-receptive managers.

Where you can find a good match between a self-sufficient analyst and a receptive line manager, by all means decentralize and hold your department heads responsible for getting results. Otherwise, you should create a central analytical staff and give it your personal attention and support, particularly during its first year.

Resource Requirements

The skilled analysts of whom we have been speaking are the primary resource needed for your productivity program. Whether they must be added or reassigned depends upon whether such people are now working in your city government. But it is essential to assign analytical talent specifically to the productivity program.

What kind of people and skills are we talking about? We have referred to some of the skills, those of industrial engineers, systems analysts, accountants.

DRAW ON A VARIETY OF SKILLS

People with training in business administration should be considered. But in the absence of any specialized training, you should be looking for people with disciplined and logical minds, capable of working a problem through to its conclusion, and people with creative imaginations who can ask penetrating questions and break free of traditional ways of viewing problems. Ideally, you will be able to form an analytical team combining many of these capacities.

Creating your own analytical staff will enable you to provide your line organizations with technical assistance when they need it. Recognize that any organization has difficulty designing, approving, and implementing changes while still discharging its regular duties. Don't ask your department managers to set improvement goals without providing them with the resources necessary to meet their goals; otherwise, their failures will outnumber their successes.

Finding new and better ways of delivering services requires a great deal of effort and attention. New ideas must be sought out, carefully tested, and evaluated, and proposed methods and procedures must be worked out in precise detail. When changes are actually made, operations must be closely monitored to determine whether the benefits expected are in fact realized. Furthermore, modifications are often necessary to accommodate unforeseen problems. All of this requires a considerable amount of time of many people in the organization and must compete with a host of other tasks necessary in managing day-to-day operations. The assistance of the special analysts can keep the productivity improvement changes from being submerged by the very real concerns of the daily routine.

How many analysts are we talking about? Obviously, creation of an analytical staff more costly than anticipated savings is the very antithesis of productivity improvement. But we are not really talking about very many people. A couple of rules of thumb: plan for one or two analysts for each project for a period of three to six months; aim for an analytical staff capability of five analysts for every 1,000 employees.

Manufacturing Industries, whose operations are often less complex than government's, spend as much as one per cent of sales on this type of analytical capability.

Productivity improvement should not be viewed as a crash program, or as a one-time effort, or as the exclusive responsibility of a specialized office or department. Rather, it is a continuing priority responsibility of all departments to find more efficient ways to deliver services.

PRODUCTIVITY IS A CONTINUING PRIORITY

You and your analytical staff should be evangelists of productivity in your government, convincing everyone in every department that productivity is his responsibility. And the analytical staff is your special resource to help everyone meet this responsibility.

While we are placing great emphasis on the development of analytical capacity, it is important to recognize that the knowledge of the employee is an under-utilized resource for productivity improvement. He knows the details of his operation and can often suggest practical changes to improve productivity. Or he can create an illusion of increased productivity without substantial change.

Involving Labor and Others

If you have already been thinking about a productivity program, you should also have been discussing it with your staff, council members, and employee representatives. If not, start today.

THERE'S A BIG WORLD OUTSIDE ...USE IT

Don't rely entirely on your own organization; ask for help from local business leaders, universities, and public interest groups. And talk to your union leaders to elicit ideas, to gain their understanding and then their cooperation. They can be particularly helpful in suggesting ideas and approaches that will help gain employee acceptance. Initial reactions are often somewhat negative, but don't become discouraged. These early discussions allow others to become participants in the program as their responses are taken into consideration during the program's formative stages.

Role of the Chief Executive

Don't expect anyone to take the initiative for you. Most line managers haven't been trained to search aggressively for new methods or to make use of outside technical or business management skills to stimulate ideas. More typically they assume a passive role, evaluating whatever proposals happen to come their way. In this kind of environment, you must supply the enthusiasm and the leadership until those below you are converted.

Prepare yourself. Be sure that you under stand the productivity concept well enough to explain it persuasively. Get a few examples worked out clearly in your mind. Look at successful new ideas in other cities, or, for that matter, successful old ideas.

You must believe - before you can expect any of your staff to believe - that productivity can be increased in all departments of your government.

Time after time, your determination is going to be tested by your own staff. You must be able to respond effectively and convincingly to any department head or supervisor who says: "We're always looking for improvements, but meanwhile we're doing the best we can." Or perhaps: "Sure we have a big backlog, but what do you expect after last year's budget cuts?" Or: "Everybody knows that we have no control over the amount of work that comes in." Or: "Yeah, I know. Isn't that what we used to call [insert name of city's last management improvement program]?'

Recognize such answers as defensive postures rather than reasoned positions, and press on for facts, real problem identification, and real improvement. Accept the *status quo* only if it is demonstrably the best way, instead of the way it's always been.

One of your major tasks will be to overcome your people's natural instinct to procrastinate, especially their desire to set aside productivity improvement because it is not critical to keeping the governmental machinery churning daily.

Productivity requires a longer range perspective than the ordinary tasks. Most productivity efforts take months of persistent effort before they pay off, and thus they are at a disadvantage in competing for staff attention with the daily crises of fires, floods, crimes, zoning, consumer complaints, and auditor reports.

How can you keep a productivity program moving in this environment? Insist on specific commitments from your department heads. Spell out and commit activities, time schedules, responsibilities.

Always obtain specific agreements at the end of each meeting as to the next steps: what is to be done, who is to do it, and when results should be ready for review. Agree on the dates for follow-up meetings and hold those meetings. Commitments may not always be met, but don't accept postponements without renewed commitments.

And keep talking. First you'll convince yourself, and then you'll convince everyone around you, that you're really serious about productivity, and that productivity is worth being serious about.

In sum, be the executive: prepare yourself; manage your program; think, talk, and act productivity.

Implementing the Program

All too often, bureaucracy seems to be long on planning and programming but short on execution. Whatever your plans and organization, you have no productivity program unless it has actual impact on the delivery of services or the cost of those services. Translate your plans into action by concentrating efforts in the following major areas:

- ➤ Systematic Analysis
- ➤ Adopting Improved Technology
- ➤ Matching Resources with Demands for Services
- ➤ Scheduling of Work
- ➤ Evaluating proposals

Systematic Analysis

Serendipity is the name of a rock group, not of a management system. There is no doubt that you or some of your staff will occasionally discover some ways to improve things that you weren't looking for. But luck comes in two kinds, good and bad, and some of your unplanned gains are going to be offset by unplanned losses. So don't rely on random circumstances to feed your productivity program. Plan your search for productivity improvement opportunities in a systematic fashion.

The following tasks are involved in systematic analysis:

- Define the objective
- Obtain the facts, identify all alternatives
- Estimate costs and benefits of each alternative
- Select the best alternative, design a model
- Specify criteria for measuring progress

Executing all these tasks may be more than is required for many of your operations, and we won't treat all of them in detail here. But the list contains some points we would like to highlight.

KNOW EXACTLY WHAT THE OBJECTIVES ARE

Clear statements of operational objectives are in- dispensable to good management. The definition should be realistic, translatable into specific work products, attainable with resources available, and as quantifiable as the nature of the work allows. A welfare department's objectives would include timely payment to all eligible recipients. A police department can set priorities for response times. A health department can set both qualitative and quantitative objectives for its inspection service.

Failure to define objectives clearly causes myriad of problems. In one sense, the point seems obvious: How can a manager proceed towards an objective when he doesn't know what it is? But the problem is not usually that no objective is stated, but that the stated objective is not managerially useful. It may provide no fixed base for planning, such as the frequently heard "maximum service at minimum cost." It may not be translatable into terms of work products.

If a prosecutor is to achieve "justice," should he work for more or fewer prosecutions, convictions, guilty pleas, cases closed? Or the objective may not be attainable, such as "elimination of all crime in the city," and not a realistic guide.

If analysis of all alternative means of attaining an objective seems to be too ambitious, start with the one you can see, that is, the way things are being done now. Have your analysts gather factual data by observing and recording what a typical employee does during each work shift, how he performs each task, and how long each task requires. Frequently used techniques for this are time-and-motion study, work sampling, and predetermined methods/time standards. The results help identify and measure losses in productivity and their probable causes. It is this type of first-hand observation that most often will indicate the nature of needed improvements. Figure 5 sets forth some of the typical cause and effect relationships uncovered by these approaches.

If there is a great deal of idle time, for instance, then scheduling may need to be improved, or perhaps the crew size is too large for the operation. If each employee spends an hour or more each day filling out reports, the information requirements may be too extensive or complex. The possibilities are almost unlimited, but the point is that a thorough study of the present use of manpower will usually pinpoint the problems to be given priority attention and often suggest the nature of the solution as well.

OBSERVE OPERATIONS FIRST HAND

Manpower utilization studies are primarily concerned with the job content and performance of each employee. They can be building blocks in broader systems analyses, which look more at the interrelationships between various functions.

Systems analysis will be concerned with the flow of information, the sequence of activities, the interrelationships of activities and their effect on the whole system. Systems analysis is usually characterized by flow diagrams that trace information flow and the sequence of activities from start to finish. These diagrams are one example of how a model of an operating system can be developed. And they aid in identifying opportunities to simplify record keeping, z expand the use of communications and data processing, reduce response times, and eliminate duplication.

These analytical approaches to productivity enable you to deal with facts rather than opinions, and with reasons, not excuses. After you obtain solid accurate facts, your key to creating improvements is systematic questioning. Nothing should be taken for granted. Each activity should be subjected to the penetrating questions such as "Why is it done, what does it accomplish, how could it be done easier?" Ideally, the end-product of every analytical study is an operating system that:

- Utilizes the most cost-effective technology available
- Applies the lowest cost mix of skills required to perform the work
- Avoids or minimizes non-productive time of each employee.

Figure 5. Common Problems of Low Productivity and Indicated Corrective Actions

Problem	Corrective Actions

Sufficient work is not available or workloads are unbalanced:

> Reallocate manpower: revise work schedules or use temporary help as needed during winter season.
>
> Change work schedules: mechanics rescheduled to second shift when equipment is not in use.
>
> Reduce crew size: collection crew size reduced from 4 to 3 men.

Lack of equipment or materials:

> Improve inventory controls: Revise reorder points to reduce stock-outs
>
> Improve distribution system: Asphalt deliveries expedited to eliminate paving delays.
>
> Improve equipment availability: Preventive maintenance program instituted.
>
> Reevaluate equipment: Obsolete trucks replaced.

Self-imposed idle time or slow work-pace:

> Train supervisors: Road maintenance foremen trained in work scheduling, dispatching, and quality control.
>
> Use performance standards: "Flat rate" manual standards adopted to measure auto mechanics performance.
>
> Schedule more work: Park maintenance crews mobilized and work scheduling system installed.

Too much time spent on non productive activities:

> Reduce excessive travel time: Permit expiration dates changed to reduce travel time of health inspectors.
>
> Reevaluate job description and task assignments: Building inspectors trained to handle multiple inspections.

Problem	Corrective Actions

Excessive manual effort required:

    Mechanize repetitive tasks: Automatic change and toll collection machines installed and toll collector staffing reduced.

Response or processing time too slow:

    Combine tasks or functions: Voucher processing and account posting combined to speed vendor payments.

    Automate the process: Computerized birth record storage and retrieval system installed.

    Improve dispatching procedures: Fire alarm patterns analyzed and equipment response policies revised.

    Revise deployment practices: Police patrol zones redefined to improve response time.

    Adopt project management techniques: Project control system installed to reduce construction cycle.

Adopting Improved Technology

The electorate that put you in office did not expect you to invent a trash compactor, design a snow plow, or build a computer. But it does expect you to see that your city is as technologically up to date as its resources will allow, and that means that you have a continuing obligation to see that your city departments are adopting whatever technology will improve their productivity.

Some technological changes simply substitute machines for men or one machine for another. The typewriter replaced the pen, and the electric typewriter replaced the manual typewriter; but all enable a person to place words on paper.

Other forms of technological improvement supplant entire processes. Airplanes have almost completely replaced trains in the transportation of passengers over long distance. It is hard for the layman to predict what form of technological change is going to take place next.

KEEP UP WITH NEW TECHNOLOGIES

Whether or not you can develop new technology, you can do several things to accelerate the rate of adoption of known techniques and products to upgrade your own productivity.

First, be sure that your department heads and their technical staffs are continually informed about new developments and applications. You have a right to expect career professional managers to be knowledgeable of the technology in their field. They should subscribe to appropriate trade journals and maintain communications with manufacturers and suppliers to be that these sources understand your particular needs.

LEARN FROM THE EXPERIENCE
OF OTHER CITIES

Your staff should also actively search out other jurisdictions where new techniques are being tried. Known disparities in the costs of providing the same services in different communities suggest that there should be greater exchange of information. Do you need park benches less vulnerable to vandalism? Can you mechanize bulk refuse collection? Are you plagued with false alarms? Does it take too long to dispatch a Patrol car? These questions have already resulted in technological improvements in some jurisdictions.

Matching Resources with Demands For Services

Resource allocations often follow patterns established years ago though demand characteristics have changed over time. As a result, employees sometimes lack work and other times cannot cope with massive backlogs. A typical example is the tax accountant, whose workload suddenly multiplies in the first quarter of each year.

Do your police and fire deployment policies match periods of high crime and fire incidence? Are mechanics available when equipment is not in use? Are vacations scheduled during periods when demands are low? Every department has unique demand characteristics that should be reexamined periodically, and manpower deployments should be modified to match the demands.

OLD HABITS DIE HARD . . . BUT THEY CAN BE KILLING YOU

On the other hand, there are many government functions whose demands can be controlled or substantially influenced by the administration. In these situations it may be easier to smooth the flow of work than to establish abnormal work schedules.

Activities keyed to expiration or renewal dates, such as permits and inspections, are of this type. Not only can these dates be rearranged to smooth the work flow, but they can also be organized according to geographical location to improve the efficiency of the work force well beyond what random demand patterns allow.

Another aspect of the resource question is the crew size required to perform activities where two or more people are assigned to work as a team, such as two-man patrol cars, inspection teams, or highway repair. Such groups are often overstaffed to accommodate absenteeism, unforeseen problems, or perhaps habits carried over from times when more manual effort was required. All such group activities should be reexamined, but don't rely on opinions to determine proper crew sizes. The contribution of each crew member and the consequences of a reduction can be determined factually and accurately through careful analysis.

Scheduling of Work

How often have you heard, or perhaps yourself said, that the big problem in government operations is the quality of first line supervision? Time and again this group has incurred the brunt of criticism regarding the poor quality of work and low efficiency of government employees. Is this criticism valid, and if so, what can be done about it? This question bears careful consideration because it gets at the very heart of the day-to-day productivity of most public employees.

Let's consider the perspective of the typical supervisor. Chances are that he is conducting himself in a manner very similar to the way he was supervised by his predecessor. Has anyone assisted him in developing a systematic way to schedule work so that it can be performed efficiently, or to develop performance standards so that he knows how much work his employees should do each day? Or is he expected to be his own industrial engineer and systems analyst?

The key point is that in contrast to industry, government expects too much of its first line supervisors and doesn't reward them for doing what it expects.

The absence of systematic work planning and scheduling is prevalent throughout government organizations. it is perhaps the greatest opportunity for productivity improvement. The very existence of a carefully prepared work schedule is the personification of effective management, for it defines what is to be done, by whom, and how much work is expected. Consequently, your productivity program will fall far short of its potential unless it aims at designing systems to organize, schedule, and dispatch work routinely and in a manner that will utilize the available resources most effectively.

Evaluating Proposals

Often you will be called upon to arbitrate between those who recommend improvements and others who resist them. A lot of time and effort will be wasted if your organization is unable to move beyond this Point.

ASK THE RIGHT QUESTIONS

How can you gauge whether a thorough study has been performed and sound recommendations presented? The following line of questioning will help you determine the depth of the analysis and the appropriateness of the proposals.

- Does the analysis show a clear understanding of the purposes of the operation under study? Do the people in the operation share this understanding?

- Does the study show what percentage of time highly skilled personnel devote to clerical or other lesser skilled tasks?

- Has the study team compared the present performance level of the employees with what should normally be achieved? If it is low, what is proposed to improve it?

- Is the study team knowledgeable about the latest technology and have they evaluated its applicability?

- Has a profile of the demands for services been constructed and matched with the deployment of resources?

If you and your analysts are asking enough of the right kind of questions, you are going to find that path to productivity improvement.

Managing Projects

While we can state a general theoretical definition of productivity-the relationship between resources used and results achieved and can make general recommendations on how to organize a productivity program, a generalized management approach will not in itself achieve the productivity improvements you are after. Practical implementation of productivity concepts will require quite different steps in different governmental activities. Trash collection must deal with the number of residences and businesses to be served; data processing must concern itself with data collection instruments and report requirements; a motor pool must keep vehicles in service. Each activity presents its own definitional and analytical problems.

To make sure each project has undergone a thorough analysis, and to keep track of your productivity program on all fronts, you and your productivity program manager should adopt a project management approach. It has several key elements:

- ➢ Project Coordinators
- ➢ Work Plans
- ➢ Status Reports
- ➢ Management Response to Problems
- ➢ Evaluation

Project Coordinators

For each productivity improvement project, assign a project coordinator. His duties will be to see that project work plans are prepared; to keep informed as to progress made and problems encountered; to see that the appropriate line managers are also kept informed and to respond promptly when problems need to be solved or decisions have to be made.

DELEGATE RESPONSIBILITY

Generally, these coordination duties can be handled on a part-time basis, or conversely, several projects can be handled by one full-time coordinator. Project coordinators should be responsible to your productivity program manager.

Work Plans

Insist on having a work plan prepared for each project, for without it you will have no effective means of getting specific commitments and of monitoring progress. Each work plan should contain the following:

- Statement of objectives
- Scope of project
- Description of the tasks to be performed
- Identification of the individuals (by name) who will be responsible for each task
- Completion date of each task.

These work plans need not be lengthy; rather they should be concise and to the point. Aside from the obvious benefit of enabling you to track progress and measure performance, the written work plan yields other advantages. Writing the work plan increases the likelihood that it will be carefully thought out. "Writing maketh the exact man." Careful definition of the scope and objectives of the plan should make it more realistic and help avoid misunderstandings.

PINPOINT RESULTS THROUGH A REGULAR REPORTING SYSTEM

Insist that the plan state what specific results are to be achieved, and see that they are stated as quantitatively as the nature of the work allows. Quantitative outputs are very important to evaluation, to which we shall return in a moment. And they clarify managerial responsibilities, continually focusing attention on the project's Main objective.

Status Reports

Periodical status reports should reflect the status of both the overall project and the specific tasks within it. Is the project on schedule? Are the tasks being completed on time? If not, why not? Is there some defect in the plan? Are the resources adequate? Are the individuals failing to perform their tasks?

Be sure the status reports are prepared and distributed regularly to interested parties at all levels of the organization. Knowing that reports pinpointing responsibility will be circulated is an added incentive for meeting schedules.

ACT ON PROBLEMS PROMPTLY

Information from the individual project status reports can be summarized to enable you to stay on top of all the productivity projects with a minimum of effort. Monthly summaries will be sufficient. They should be prepared by all department heads and addressed to you. Your productivity program manager should provide a standard format so that reports from ail departments can be readily reviewed.

An aggressive productivity program will flush many difficult problems to the surface, and when your reports bring them to your attention, you should discuss and resolve them with the program manager. If your reporting system is not identifying problems, then you should be concerned that your productivity program is not getting the results you want.

Management Response to Problems

You will have demonstrated your leadership by establishing the productivity program in the first place. You must continue to show your leadership and your commitment to productivity by resolving problems as they arise in your productivity projects. In addition, stir things up each month by selecting one or two projects that are behind schedule and demanding to know exactly what is being done about them.

If necessary, bring all the participants together and debate the issues until a specific decision is reached and specific action agreed upon.

Evaluation

Project status reports tell you whether or not projects are being carried out. But you still need to know whether the project is any good. To make that judgment, you need data on the specific results being achieved. As noted earlier, the place to start worrying about this problem is the project plan. The plan should identify quantitative output units that will best measure progress toward the project's objectives. For example, if your police department has a project to relieve uniformed patrolmen of routine clerical assignments that confine them to the precinct house, count the number of patrolmen or man-hours per week reassigned to patrol duty. If the health department aims to reduce time to fill requests for birth certificates, then average processing time would be an appropriate unit of measure.

Properly chosen output measures are very valuable management tools. They enable you to establish project targets and to monitor progress towards them. They also give you a concrete way to determine whether the project improvements are up to your expectations.

Evaluative data can be reported concisely using a format such as that shown in Figure 6. Quarterly evaluative reports should be sufficient, although you may prefer to see them each month.

Figure 6. Productivity Program Progress Report

PRODUCTIVITY PROGRAM PROGRESS REPORT

AGENCY _____

PROGRAM-FUNCTION	UNIT OF MEASURE	FY 1972-1973	FY 1973-1974 TARGET		FIRST QUARTER			SECOND QUARTER			THIRD QUARTER			FOURTH QUARTER			REMARKS
					JULY	AUG	SEPT	OCT	NOV	DEC	JAN	FEB	MAR	APR	MAY	JUNE	
				TARGET													
				ACTUAL													
				% OF TARGET													
				TARGET													
				ACTUAL													
				% OF TARGET													
				TARGET													
				ACTUAL													
				% OF TARGET													
				TARGET													
				ACTUAL													
				% OF TARGET													
				TARGET													
				ACTUAL													
				% OF TARGET													
				TARGET													
				ACTUAL													
				% OF TARGET													
				TARGET													
				ACTUAL													
				% OF TARGET													
				TARGET													
				ACTUAL													
				% OF TARGET													

PAGE ____ OF ____

Labor Relations

From all that we have said so far, you can see that productivity improvement must affect and involve the employee. Therefore, it is inevitable that the issue of productivity will thread its way into your relationship with labor and eventually into the collective bargaining process.

Because of the weight given to precedents in labor relations, the initial practices with respect to what is bargain able, how the bargaining is conducted, and how disputes will be settled can have longstanding consequences. You should be quite conscious of these potential consequences as you begin your productivity program, and you should be particularly concerned about maintaining good channels of communication between management and labor.

The key issues to consider fall into the following categories:
- ➢ Job Security
- ➢ Job Satisfaction
- ➢ Collective Bargaining
- ➢ Wage Incentives

Like the business executive, you are responsible for effective use of financial resources. But, as a public official, you are also obligated to consider the social consequences of your employment and personnel practices. While your productivity program addresses your responsibility as custodian of public funds, you should also be sensitive to some serious employee concerns, the foremost of which is job security.

Job Security

Will your employees believe that a productivity improvement program threatens their job security? They certainly will, because productivity improvement often means reallocation or reduction of resources, and manpower is your major resource.

Historically, manpower dislocations have resulted from technological innovations and other productivity advances. For instance, expanding use of computers has increased the need for data processing skills and reduced the need for manual and clerical skills. And in trash collection, larger equipment and automated systems have reduced the number of sanitation workers needed. Employees are aware of this process, particularly as it has taken place in their own kind of work, and their perception of it is likely to differ from yours,

Suppose that your park department is understaffed. Mechanized litter cleanup equipment or a more efficient manpower deployment may free resources which you can shift to park maintenance functions that are presently neglected. But what happens if you shift these newfound resources to some altogether different city activity? What to you is a reallocation of resources then becomes, to the employees directly affected, a reduction in force.

Keep in mind that a single layoff can have devastating personal consequences for the individual involved and can undermine the morale of the remaining workers. Fear of losing jobs can be the dominant force that motivates employees to resist improvement efforts. Unfortunately, the mere mention of the word productivity is often sufficient to stir thoughts of budget cuts and layoffs.

The goal of your program is to increase productivity, not to reduce the work force. And you cannot tell at the outset exactly what course of action will increase productivity in any given case. The solution may be redesign of work methods or reassignment of tasks. It may be change in the flow or sequence of the work. Or it may be to add resources where a unit has not been able to keep pace with increasing demands.

When overstaffing does turn out to be the problem, there are alternatives to layoffs: employees should be retrained and reassigned to other programs within the scope of their interests and capabilities; and where staff reductions are necessary, they can often be made through normal attrition. It is useful to remember in this context that many productivity improvements have been necessitated by the impossibility of recruiting people to perform additional tasks.

Actual experience in local government indicates that productivity improvements rarely result in layoffs because the alternatives just discussed usually suffice. To the extent that you make use of them, you can mitigate your employees' fears and gain their cooperation.

Admittedly, productivity poses difficult labor relations problems. New approaches and new solutions are needed, and you and your peers are going to have to find them. You may need to reappraise your civil service regulations, and devote more time and money to training and development programs that will broaden employee skills and enhance their economic value. You may also need to go beyond the annual budget cycle in planning manpower requirements.

In the long run, better planning of staffing levels, job skills, and educational requirements can help alleviate these difficulties. Your productivity program can be immensely helpful in determining the real manpower needs of each department.

The responsibility for employee welfare doesn't fall entirely on your shoulders, though. Leaders of public employee unions have an equal share of responsibility in this matter. They can be particularly helpful in removing some of the constraints imposed by narrowly prescribed seniority rules. Retraining and reassignment concepts are of little practical use where employees lose all of their seniority when moved from one department to another or one bargaining unit to another.

Job Satisfaction

The employee becomes self-confident when he knows that he can routinely meet the requirements of his job. Improving productivity means change, and change arouses feelings of insecurity and fears of the unknown. Be sure to involve as many employees as possible in discussions about new ideas or new methods before they are implemented, and reassure them that they will be able to acclimate to a different way of working. And make sure all of the employees receive adequate instruction, and formal training if necessary, in their new tasks.

Productivity can be beneficial to the employee in several ways. The most important is that it is the measure of the worth of his services to the public. Productivity gains are gains in his value and grounds for increases in compensation.

Furthermore, greater productivity should result in greater ease, safety, and efficiency in the performance of the job, and these are important elements of job satisfaction. Of course, the greatest element of job satisfaction is the feeling that the job is worth doing, and any job worth doing is worth doing better.

Collective Bargaining

Collective bargaining of wages, employee benefits, and working conditions is a complex phenomenon that is as dependent on local circumstances as it is on general economic conditions, and productivity improvement will be but one of many issues to be considered.

Nevertheless, the productivity program can provide you the information you need about how work is actually performed and how you want to modify it. Wherever work schedules, deployment patterns, and other work rules are constraints to greater efficiency or work quality, you will be better prepared to negotiate these issues. Whether or not proposed changes need to be negotiated, always discuss them with employee representatives before you implement them. And be willing to accept suggestions that don't adversely affect your primary objectives.

From organized labor's point of view, productivity represents an opportunity for employees to share the economic benefits of greater productivity. And they will also expect a voice in how change takes place.

You represent the public interest in collective bargaining, and you should continually strive for recognition by labor of their public responsibility to cooperate in productivity improvement efforts. Find common grounds here both management and labor share similar objectives and your program should move forward without major confrontation.

Recognize, however, that collective bargaining alone will not make your organization more productive. In the final analysis management must still define the work to be done, and how, when, and by whom, it is to be done. It is still your responsibility to effectively manage all of the resources at your disposal.

And you cannot bargain away your responsibility for productivity; the public holds you accountable for the results.

Wage Incentives

Productivity is often linked to employee motivation, and wage incentives have long been used in industry to motivate employees to higher performance. The subject will almost certainly arise during the course of your productivity program. But proceed with caution.

There are many pitfalls in using public funds for incentive pay purposes. Can the integrity of an incentive plan be maintained over the long haul as policies change and technology advances? Will the data upon which payments are based be recorded or verified by participants or by non-participants? Can quality be controlled where earnings are based solely on the quantity of work done? And what will be the consequences as inequities arise between incentive and non-incentive jobs? These are difficult questions, indeed, and there is little precedent to guide you.

The National Commission on Productivity and Work Quality has recently reported on several approaches being tried in state and local governments around the country (Managing Human Resources in Local Government: A Survey of Employee Incentives, National Commission on productivity, October, 1973).

These haven't yet stood the test of time. So assign a member of your staff to search out the various approaches being tried; to identify the problems encountered; and to determine what benefits are being achieved.

Incentives can increase employees, receptivity to change, and they can motivate employees to be more effective in executing the tasks that are assigned to them by their supervisors. On the other hand, you cannot depend on individual workers to develop new technology, coordinate delivery of services involving many different jobs, or determine how and when each task should be performed.

In short, there are many techniques to increase productivity, and a wage incentive program is but one.

IMPROVE YOUR WORK METHODS FIRST

Wage incentives should only be considered after work methods and practices have been carefully analyzed and the best practical methods of operation developed and installed. Methods improvements should come first. So don't wait to decide about wage incentives before you begin your productivity program.

Producing for
the Public

Governmental productivity is inescapably a political responsibility. After all, what we are discussing here is how public officials spend public funds to deliver public goods and services - the most fundamental purposes and activities of government.

Productivity as such is not a salient political issue to most people, and it won't be unless basic services fail or become too expensive. Nevertheless, public confidence in the capabilities of government to perform its functions is not as strong as it should be. The citizen is aware that government is the fastest growing sector of the economy, but he is not convinced that benefits are growing as fast as outlays. A recent survey by the National Commission on Productivity and Work Quality shows that public opinion rates government workers as far less productive than many other groups of workers in the economy. Improving productivity can be a means of improving confidence in your government. How do you get public interest in and support for productivity in the absence of a crisis?

Obviously, the public has to know about your program before it can support it. And it has to see some tangible results before it can get very excited. This suggests a careful laying of the foundations for public support. Until your program has produced some demonstrable benefits, limit your public statements to comments about the need for improving productivity and your intentions to do whatever is necessary to achieve it. Show your understanding of the significance of the concept. But don't oversell a program before it has any real substance.

When you begin your productivity program, invite your local reporters to a background briefing, but again, don't oversell. Your objective at this point is to give them a basis for understanding how you intend to proceed and what you hope to achieve, telling them in effect how you want to have your administration evaluated.

Making specific plans and subsequent evaluation reports public entails some risk, but planning, evaluation, and problem solution are creditable enterprises and the public should be aware of them. Also, contrast the risks of candor to the risks of remaining silent about recognizable problems. You can also use the visibility of the program as additional motivation for the employees involved. Publicizing specific data on performance, provided it is reliable and identifies problems as well as achievements, will enhance the credibility of the program.

Favorable results, of course, are by far the best marketing device. Document and publicize specific, tangible examples of productivity gains.

Give credit to those who have achieved the gains. Employee awards - promotions, raises, commendations, certificates of achievement - are an excellent means of drawing attention to productivity improvement while simultaneously recognizing outstanding work.

Arrange public demonstrations of technological improvements such as new fire fighting equipment, communications systems, or crime prevention techniques. Make use of every opportunity for public education. Let the public know how its cooperation can help cut costs or improve services. And you and your staff should include comments on the program whenever you address local public interest groups.

Your basic message is always the same. Your government is serious about managing the public resources efficiently. Productivity improvement shows your dedication to giving the public the most for its money.

*   *   *   *

Author's Notes

So Mr. Mayor . . . was written for the National Commission on Productivity and Work Quality. Prior to this undertaking I was manager of the productivity improvement program for the City of New York (official title: Deputy Director of the Budget) during John V. Lindsay's second mayoral term.

New York City was experiencing a severe budget shortfall such that improving the productivity of every municipal department had become imperative.

Perhaps the greatest opportunity to streamline municipal operations was to apply advanced technology, especially interactive computing. New York City was a world leader in applying computers to advance government productivity. For instance, the Police Department developed the first automated crime analysis program to identify crime patterns and to strategically deploy patrols to interrupt those patterns.

So Mr. Mayor . . . was initially printed by the U.S. Government Printing Office (Pub. No. NCOP 7501). It was intentionally oversized (11" by 11") so that it could not easily be misplaced and forgotten on a mayoral book shelf. It has long been out-of-print, and alas mostly forgotten. So much for good intentions! Nevertheless the productivity message it conveys is timeless - in fact it seems to be more urgent than ever.

Here it is republished in the hope that it may prevent "reinventing the wheel", or at least minimizing such reinventions.